CCSS **Genre** Fiction

 Essential Question
What can we see in the sky?

A Special Sunset

by Loretta Wilcox

illustrated by Jeremy Tugeau

Maria and Dad are at
the **airport**.

They will take a plane.
It will be an **adventure**!

Maria has **dreamed** of flying. She can't wait to get on.

The plane is **late**! Maria is upset. She turns away. But Dad points to the window.

Maria sits by the window.
Soon, the plane takes off.

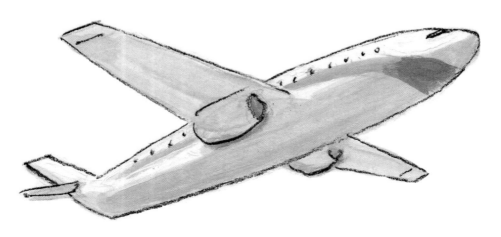

The plane flies high in the sky. Maria likes to look out.

Maria sees **clouds**. The sun
is setting. Its light makes
them **glow**.

They fly past trees. They fly past lakes. They fly past houses.

But they do not fly past
the **sunset**!

Maria says, "Dad, the sun is still setting. Why aren't we flying past it?"

"The things on Earth are much closer to us," says Dad. "So we pass them quickly as we fly."

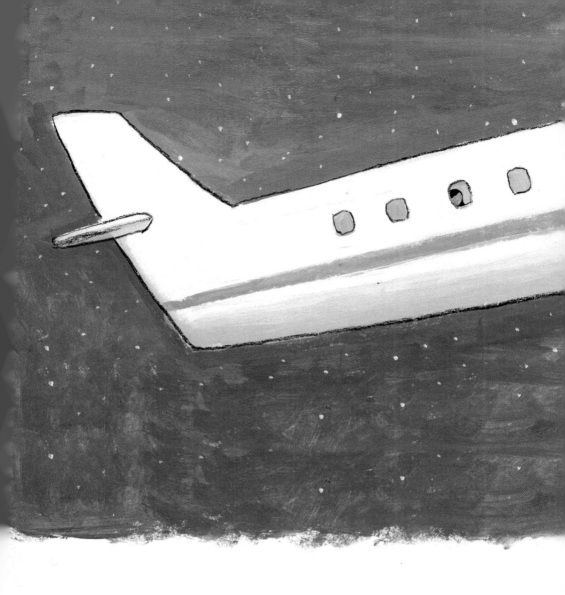

Maria nods. "The sun is very far away," she says. "So it takes longer to pass."

The plane flies on. At last,
the sun sets.

Maria looks out. Now, they
will follow the moon!

Respond to Reading

Summarize

Summarize *A Special Sunset.* Use the chart to help you.

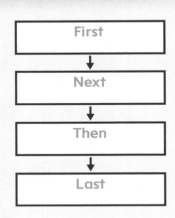

First
↓
Next
↓
Then
↓
Last

Text Evidence

1. What happens after Maria sees the sunset? Sequence

2. Reread page 5. How can you tell what *upset* means from the words and pictures? Vocabulary

3. Write about what you think Maria will see next.

   Write About Reading

Compare Texts
Read about what the sun's light can do on the ground.

Shadows and Sundials

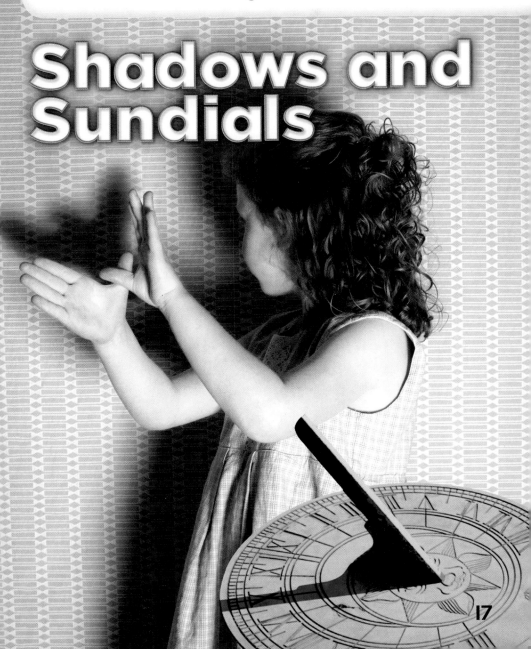

You have a shadow. Everyone does. You can play games with shadows. You can make shadow animals. You can also use shadows to tell time.

Sundials are the oldest way to tell time. They work because shadows have a pattern. They move from one side of an object to the other as the sun moves. The shadow on the sundial tells the time.

Make Connections

How does the sun help the sundial tell time? Essential Question

How does movement affect both the sunset and the sundial?

Text to Text

Focus on
Literary Elements

Plot The plot tells what happens in a story. The events are in order: first, next, then, last.

What to Look for In *A Special Sunset*, a girl flies on a plane. First, the girl goes to the airport. Next, the plane takes off. Then she sees things out the window.

Your Turn

Think about flying on a plane. What would you see? Tell the things you would see in order. Use the words *first, next, then,* and *last.*